The
Little Book
of
Witchcraft

Written
By
Nigel D. Salmon

CONTENTS

Introduction

Before learning how to do witchcraft, it is very important that you first learn some basic rules about being a witch. These rules are important to your survival and effectiveness. So study them and apply them. Here are six rules:

1. **You must completely believe in ghosts and demons.**

To practice witchcraft, you must believe that ghosts and demons exist and that they have powers to make things happen. You will have to believe in spiritualism. Without the belief in ghosts and demons, you cannot be a witch. Remember, you will rely on ghosts and demons to carry out curses, haunting, protection, etc. If you do not believe in ghosts and demons, then you should forget about being a witch.

2. **Continue learning the use of the two main weapons.**

Witchcraft consists of two main weapons—spirits and potions. How well you learn to use them will determine how effective you are as a witch.

3. <u>Learn one thing at a time.</u>

You should not attempt to learn everything about witchcraft at once. This can get you confused. So start with one thing at a time. As you go along, you should learn from experience. Remember, there are two main weapons in witchcraft—spirits and potions.

When you are learning the use of spirits, you will learn the following:

- Types of spirits
- Identifying the activities of a demon from a ghost
- Invocation
- Exorcism
- Instructing spirits

When you are learning the use of potions, you will learn:

- Purpose (or purposes) of the potion
- How to make it
- How it should be used
- It's effects
- And—if applicable—the antidote against it

Don't worry; you will learn these inside this book. So simply read on.

4. <u>Do not use your powers as entertainment.</u>

You should not learn witchcraft and then go about showing off your powers.   Becoming a witch is not the same as becoming a magician. A magician will develop and learn tricks to entertain. A magician is an entertainer. A witch is not. A magician uses tricks, but a witch uses real spirits and potions.

5. You should keep a low profile.

It is not a matter of fear why you should keep a low profile. It is a matter of being judicious. By not attracting unnecessary attention to yourself, you will find it rather easier and safer to exercise your powers without drawing suspicion from others. For example: If you will have to invoke a spirit and instruct it to possess an enemy so that he or she commits suicide—you would not want to do this with everyone knowing that you are the one responsible for it. So you should keep a low profile and do not brag about your powers.

6. Protect yourself and the innocent

It is not a good idea to learn witchcraft merely to harm and kill. You should learn witchcraft to protect yourself and the innocent. With the use of witchcraft, you can protect yourself and others from harmful and destructive events.

7. Exercise what you have learned.

To gain magical powers, you cannot only read about witchcraft. In order to gain magical powers, you must exercise the things you have learned. So do not only read this book. You must do what it says.

Questions and Answers

<u>Can witchcraft protect me from getting killed by an enemy?</u>

Yes. If your enemy wants to attack you using spirits, you should protect yourself using spirits equally strong, or stronger, to the enemy's.

If those who want to kill you are relying on the use of guns, knives or other tangible weapons, your self defence should also rely on divination. If you are unable to divine (predict coming dangers) there will be limitation in defending yourself. To effectively protect yourself from getting killed by a tangible weapon, you should either:

(a) Avoid the enemy by relying on a spirit of divination. You will learn about spirits of divination later in this book.

(b) Eliminate the potential attacker using spirits. This can be done by instructing the spirit to cause the individual to meet in an accident, hallucinate, go mad, or die. If you are under attack and will have to act on the spot, a wise thing to do is to cause the attacker to hallucinate. Hallucinations can be caused by a potion or spirit. Spirits under your command will show themselves to the attacker as replicas of you or show themselves as some kind of frightening creatures. Another thing you can do (if you are working with demons) is to let the spirits madden the attacker. This means the spirits will slap the individual, which will make him mad, or possess him so he will go and kill himself.

Can I use witchcraft to cure an illness?

Yes, depending on what the illness is. In witchcraft, there are healing potions for a lot of things—such as constipation, allergies and many forms of infections and poisons.

If an individual is ill due to possession by a spirit, such person can be cured by an act of witchcraft. You will learn how this is done later in this book.

How do I get the power of foretelling?

Ability of foretelling can be obtained through different methods. To foretell, the best way is to allow your self to be possessed by a 'demon of divination'. Such a demon will reveal to you future events and secret occurrences.

What happens when someone is possessed by a demon?

Different demons have different effects on those they possess. What happens when someone is possessed depends on the kind of demon, the amount of demons, or the intent behind the demon possessing the person.

Can I use witchcraft to turn a person into an animal?

Yes. You can turn yourself or another person into an animal (example: a frog). You can also turn a stone or other object into a particular creature. There are two ways to do this (a) spirits only or (b) spirits and potions. But first you will have to learn how to use spirits and potions, as this book will show.

Can witchcraft cause cancer?

No. Someone cannot use witchcraft to give someone else cancer. However, a curse put on someone's body through witchcraft can present syndromes very similar to some named diseases.

Can anyone learn witchcraft?

Anyone who is able to learn should be able to learn witchcraft. A person should be dedicated to the learning process.

How different is a ghost from a demon?

A ghost is the spirit of an individual which leaves the body at death. A demon, on the other hand, is a spirit that was once an angel.

Demons are far more powerful than ghosts. A demon can directly kill someone.   Demons can rip off tree branches, turn over tables and chairs, fly someone through the air, move or fling stones, cause someone's body part to rot, stir large body of water, start a fire, form in the likeness of humans and things, and even cause an earthquake.

A ghost can show itself in the likeness as when it was alive. It can cause someone to die, cause someone to go mad; or create sounds to haunt.

Terms and Definitions

Bath
This is the act of a witch bathing a client. The act is considered to 'wash away bad luck or harmful influences'.

Witchcraft
The evil and good use of magic powers

Demon
A spirit which was once an angel

Devil or Satan
The chief and most powerful demon

Divination
The use of supernatural means to find out about the future or the unknown

Black magic
Magic used for harmful purposes.

White magic
Magic used for good purposes.

Incantation
A magic spell or a charm.

Evince
To evince is 'to reveal the presence of'. A witch may be able to evince (reveal the presence of) a   spirit

inside an individual or place.

Exorcism
The act of removing a spirit from controlling a person or existing in a place.

Invocation
The act of calling on a ghost or demon.

Ritual
A ceremony.

Magical object
An object used as aid in the practice of magic.

Séance
A meeting to make contact with the dead.

Magical Words
Words used to enable effects of magic.

Potion
A mixture (drink, powder, etc.) with healing, magical, or poisonous power.

Medium
A means to communicate with the dead.

Curse
Harm, death or misery engendered by an appeal to a supernatural power.

Imprecation
A spoken curse.

Mind control
The term used to describe the act of controlling the

behaviour of someone via a potion or spirit, or the use of both.

Spirit potion
A potion used in combination with a spirit or spirits.

Dealing with spirits

The power to deal with spirits lies in words called
<u>magical words</u>. There are two types of magical words.
The first type uses an old or unnamed language,
which makes it impossible for the general public to
understand. Below is an example of this type. This
one calls upon a demon.

Xemus Plutos of darkness
Summon Quantus Mius.

The other type is written or spoken in your own
language. This is the type that this book will teach
you on. Ok, so let's continue.

You will use magical words to call on a spirit and
then command it to act. The magical words are not
the same in different situations. The situation to be
dealt with and the command or request that will have
to be made, will determine the very words to be used.
However, words do not become magical words by
merely putting some words together. Magical words
must do two basic things, as follows:

(a) Call on a spirit and

(b) Tell it what to do.

These two elements must exist for magical words to have success. Along with the words you articulate, you will have to at times use the aid of an object to perform an entire ritual to have the desired result in certain situation.

The following are situations in which one deals with spirits:

Invocation

Invocation is the first and main step for all persons when dealing with spirits. When dealing with a spirit, a witch has to invoke. But before performing an invocation, you must have a purpose. You should not perform an invocation merely out of curiousity. There are different methods of invocations. So here are some of the methods.

Invocation by a séance

You can invoke a spirit through a séance. In fact, invocation is the main purpose of a séance. A séance is a meeting to make contact with the dead. A séance might not work in the first meeting. Sometimes you will have to perform a séance more than one time before you get a response from the targeted spirit. You may perform a séance the first night, second night and then on the third night, the ghost responds. The act takes patience.

Rules of a séance

To perform a séance, you must know these simple rules:

(a) One person cannot perform a séance. There must be two are more persons to perform the act.

(b) The persons who will perform the séance should know the full name of the dead that will be summoned. If the name of the dead is not known, it should be summoned by calling it 'spirit'.

(c) The séance should be performed either at the tomb of the deceased, the place the dead is haunting, or in the presence of a person the dead individual loves or is haunting.

(d) The séance must be performed in the absence of bright light, noise or any other distraction. Therefore it is best to perform it late in the evening or night.

(e) To have order, the séance should have a leader. The leader (someone with the required knowledge or experience) is the one who will lead the group and accommodate the dead on its arrival.

(f) The person performing the séance must sit or stand close together, preferably in a circle holding hands.

Purpose of the séance

There must be a purpose. The two main purposes for performing a séance are: (1) to stop a spirit that is haunting a person or place (2) to merely communicate with a spirit.

How to perform a séance

As stated above, there are two main purposes for performing a séance. The purpose will determine the method, as follows:

Method One: If the purpose for performing the séance is to stop a spirit from haunting a person or place, the group should perform the act by inviting the spirit into the séance (meeting) and then instruct it to go back into the spirit realm. How you will instruct the spirit will depend on the behaviour of the spirit. If the spirit is haunting by merely showing itself to selected persons now and again, the instruction should be rather friendly—because this might just be a spirit that is not at rest. It might be the spirit of someone who was not ready to die or who has not crossed over completely into the spirit realm. In this case, the leader of the séance should not drive the spirit away when it is called into the séance. Instead, the idea should be to put the spirit to rest. On the other hand, if the spirit is violent or destructive, the séance must be performed to attract the spirit and then drive (force) it away.

Method Two: If the purpose of a séance is to invite and talk with a ghost, the way to do it is to let the leader of the séance become a medium. This means that the leader of the séance will allow the spirit to enter him in order for the ghost to have a voice to speak. Remember, a ghost does not have a voice box. So it has to use something or someone with a voice box in order to speak with the living. While the ghost is speaking through the leader of the séance, the leader may take on one or more of the characteristics of such spirit.

What to bring to a séance

There are different things that are used to aid the success of a séance. Some things are requisite while others are optional. The requisite things are: full or semi darkness, belief in the process, silence (no unnecessary talking or sound), and the rules previously stated. The optional things are: candles, a skull, glasses of water, something belonging to the deceased, or Ouija board.

What to say at a séance

When performing a séance to stop a ghost making appearances in a place, the following is an example of what to say. Let's say the name of the deceased is Mandy Lewis:

(The leader says the following):

"Mandy Lewis, we know you are here.
Mandy, we come as your friend.
We ask you to join us now.
Mandy, we invite you into our circle."

(Everyone must now repeat the following until the ghost arrives):

"Spirit of Mandy Lewis, come into our circle."

So how will you know when the spirit arrives? The spirit will manifest itself either visually or by doing something. So everyone in the group must look out and listen for anything strange—such as the sound of something moving. Remember, when a ghost manifests itself visually this may occur in a very short space of time—like four seconds, for example. On the arrival of the ghost the leader should immediately instruct it as follows:

"Mandy Lewis, we know you are not at rest.
So I speak to you as a friend.
Obey my voice, Mandy.
From this circle I command you to leave this place.
Be gone from this place and never return! Leave this place!"

At this time everyone in the group must keep silent for about a minute. And if nothing happens during this time, break the silence. You can break a séance by simply ending it.

-- ----- ------

If the purpose of the séance is to talk with the spirit of a deceased, the following is an example of what to say. Let's say the name of the deceased is Duke Ellis and the names of his parents are John and Betsy Ellis.

The invitation of the ghost can begin as follows:

(The leader says the following):

"We are here to invite the spirit of Duke Ellis."

(The group must repeat the following, about six times):

"Spirit of Duke Ellis, we invite you into our circle."

(The leader alone now persuades the ghost to come, as follows):

"Duke Ellis, son of John and Betsy Ellis, I hereby invite you into my soul.
Speak through me."

(The group must now repeat the following, like before):

"Spirit of Duke Ellis, we invite you into our circle."

The leader of the séance must say anything that will persuade the spirit to enter him, but everyone else in the group should keep to the repeating of this line:

"Spirit of Duke Ellis, we invite you into our circle."

When the spirit arrives, it will begin speaking through the leader. You <u>should not</u> expect to see some of the same things you see in a movie.   For example, the leader's voice will not change.   However, changes in the leader's behaviour and facial expression will be evidence of the ghost's presence in him.

At this point the leader is not in control of the group. Someone else from the group must now speak directly to the spirit (Duke Ellis) that is inside the leader. The person must speak directly to the spirit, not the leader. The conversation with the spirit should be short, at most ten minutes or less, so as to not keep the spirit inside the leader for long.

To ensure the leader is not pretending, ask a simple question that the deceased knows the answer to but the leader doesn't.

Before breaking the séance, someone in the group must drive the spirit from the leader. If someone does not drive the spirit from the leader, the leader could become non compos mentis (insane). The spirit can be driven out as follows:

"Duke Ellis, I now command you to leave our presence. Return to the place from which you came. Leave his body now!"

<u>Note</u>: The spirit should leave the body of the leader at the breaking of the séance. But as a precaution, it is wise to drive out the spirit before breaking the séance.

Invocation At A Tomb

You can invoke a spirit by visiting a tomb. This is an invoking method popular in Haiti, Jamaica, and parts of Africa. To carry out the act, you will need a long iron and special oil. A simple alternative to the oil is animal blood. The oil or animal blood is to appease the spirit, thus preventing it from harming you. After meeting these requirements, the next step is to call up a ghost.

So let's say that the spirit of a deceased named Dorothy Smith will be invoked. You would begin the procedure by rubbing yourself with the oil, or animal blood, and then get ready with the long iron. At the tomb, you would call on the ghost in the likely following words:

"Dorothy Smith, Dorothy Smith,
I call on you from your resting place."

Then you would thrust her coffin once and repeat the call and thrust of the coffin 3 more times.

If the spirit did not respond after the above procedure was done, you would be more detailed in the calling as follows:

"Dorothy Smith, Dorothy Smith, daughter of (name of her parent) I call upon you.
Dorothy Smith, I summon your spirit unto me.
Hear me now and come up from among the dead."

You would repeat these words at least three times and thrust her coffin with the long iron between each repeat. When the ghost responds you should know this when you see the ghost or hear a sound/voice. During the manifestation of the ghost, you should not run away. At this time, without delay, you must utilize the second element of your magical words—which is to command the ghost to act. Exact what you want the ghost to do will help you decide what to say.

For the sake of completing the example hereof, let's assume that the ghost of Dorothy Smith will be sent to affect a serial killer named Jacob Hanson so that he will die. You should instruct the ghost as follows:

"Spirit of Dorothy Smith, I know you.
Act to my command as I now instruct you.
Jacob Hanson of (his address) you must now destroy.
Make three attempts on his life to cut him off.
Afterwards, return to where I called you from I now command".

Note: The second part of your magical words must be spoken clearly, because it is the part that gives the ghost instruction to act. Clearly, you must tell the ghost that you 'know' it—which helps to let the ghost accepts you and be willing to obey you.   The ghost is then told 'how many times' it should make an attempt on Jacob Hanson's life   and then, importantly, it should return to where you have called it from. If the ghost is not successful in its three attempts to destroy Jacob Hanson, it will not make any more attempts. It will go back to its place, as instructed in the words.

Why three attempts? You give the ghost three attempts—in case the first attempt fails. Do not go more than three attempts.

Note that if you want to use the ghost again, you should not instruct it to return to the spirit realm. Instead, the instruction must be for the ghost to return to you. If not, you will have to go back to the tomb to invoke the ghost of Dorothy Smith again or to another tomb to bring up another ghost.

The intention to use the ghost more than once means you would have to change the second element of the magical words (the part telling the ghost what to do) to something as follows:

"Spirit of Dorothy Smith, I know you.
Act to my command as I now instruct you.
Jacob Hanson of (Jacob Hanson address) you must now befall. Make three attempts on his life to cut him off. Afterwards bring yourself back to me and stay at the voice of my command."

If you keep the ghost of Dorothy Smith at your place or with you, you would now become a witch and can go on to use the ghost any time at the snap of your fingers. By having the ghost, you can develop very simple ways of calling it and instructing it to act.   It would be like having a new dog. The longer you are together, the easier the instructions get.

Interestingly, the spirit of Dorothy Smith will not leave you unless you put it back (command it to go back). You can now invoke other spirits without having to go 'their' graves. To do so, you will simply send the ghost of Dorothy Smith to go and bring forth such spirits. For example: say you live in Kingston, Jamaica. Someone from Bridgetown, Barbados comes to you with request for you to bring up the spirit of a little girl buried back in Barbados. Now, you do not have to travel to the tomb of the little girl in Barbados to bring her spirit up. Because you have the spirit of Dorothy Smith with you, all you will have to do is instruct the ghost of Dorothy Smith to bring forth the spirit of the little girl. And yes, the spirit of the girl can be brought forth within seconds or minutes.

Sometimes your ghost may be unable to bring forth other ghosts. Some spirits might be too strong against yours. You may want to bring forth a spirit from a place but cannot do so, because that spirit is stronger than the one you are using.

In order to be very strong and more effective, spiritually, you must now use the ghost of Dorothy Smith to gather unto yourself more ghosts and keep these ghosts in your control until you have an amount you consider enough. All the ghosts, along with the ghost of Dorothy Smith, will carry out instructions from you. Under your instructions, they will carry out acts of curses, haunting, espionage, killing, exorcism, protection, etc.

Invoking A Demon

Invoking a demon is not the same as invoking a ghost. The invocations are different. Demons are not spirits of the dead. They were generated in the exact form that they are presently in. Extreme caution must be taken when dealing with one or more of them. You should not merely invoke any demon and let it possess you. If you allow 'any' demon to possess (come inside of) you, the demon could be of a sort that could make you mad. When a wrong demon is inside a person, that person's behaviour will be altered to an extent. Only demons to foretell can be inside a person and be the least altering to the character of such person. Most other demons—due to their potent natures—tend to alter the behaviour of those they possess.

When dealing with demons, a person should understand five basic rules, which are:

1 .Never wear white or colourful clothing when invoking demons. It is best to wear black clothing or be nude.

2. Never use a bright light when invoking a demon. You should use the light of the full moon or lights from candles.

3. No human can see demons in their raw forms. So never request a demon to show itself. However, a demon can be considered 'visible' when it makes a deceptive appearance of something.

4. Never attempt to govern a demon. No person by his or herself has the power to rule a demon. You cannot rule a demon—you work with it. The expression: "You are my master as I am yours" shows mutual respect between a witch and a demon.

5. Never attempt to influence a demon against another demon, notwithstanding the situation you would be dealing with. If a person is possessed by an unwanted demon, you can remove the demon by invoking it out of the person. You should not try to drive the demon out with another demon. You cannot use a demon against another demon. It will not work.

Types of demons

There are different types of demons existing. Demons are simply demons but like humans, they vary in nature. They vary mainly by the powers they exude. Therefore it is possible to categorize them base on these qualities as follows:

Blood Demons

These are the sort of demons that can be invoked and exorcised with the use of blood.   When invoking a Blood Demon, you will rely on its like for blood to attract it. The blood should be from an animal.

However, blood alone does not attract such demons. To successfully invoke a Blood Demon, you have to be accompanied by:

1. Blood

2. Magical words (written or improvised)

3. A dark room with lit candles lined in a circle, in which you must stand.

4. Entirely black clothes or be nude.

To begin the invocation process, you should wait until it is late in the night and select a place that is silent and not clustered. After dressing yourself in completely black clothing, you should light the candles in a row that forms a circle. Twelve candles should be sufficient. You should now stand in the middle of the row of candles with the live animal (preferably a bird) whose blood will be used in the ritual. The next two things you should do are to utter your magical words while kill and sprinkle the animal's blood within the circle of the candles. You should not step out of the circle. When a Blood Demon arrives, you will know when strange things start occurring in your presence.

Full Moon Demons

These are the sort of demons that are aroused by the full moon. Persons and animals that they possess will act slightly eerie at the times of the full moon. Full

Moon Demons are benign. They usually do not harm persons possessed by them or cause such persons to harm others. A Full Moon Demon will stay inside a person lifelong, usually from infancy, and will move on to another human body at the death of the prior person. Because they usually house themselves inside an individual from young age, they are usually overlooked.

The exorcism of a Full Moon Demon from an individual is the easiest of all exorcisms. One way for such exorcism to work is that the person carrying the demon must first accept and then believe he or she is carrying the demon. For a person to know he or she is carrying a Full Moon Demon, it may require someone else of experience to identify the demonic behaviour. The person carrying the demon must then resist such behaviour using the power of will (preferably via a ritual of will power) until he or she roots the demon out.

If the collaboration of the person carrying the demon cannot be obtained, the demon can be removed by invoking it out during the full moon. But the procedure involves restraining the individual. So it will not be explained here.

Demons of Divination

While all demons can possess humans, not all demons give the ability to foretell the future and the unknown. The demons that foretell are herein called Demons of Divination.

Demons of Divination tend to house themselves inside persons with or without invitation. In some cases, Demons of Divination housed themselves in persons from childhood and usually become active around adolescence. Such persons will know they have supernatural abilities (but may not recognize the powers as demonic) when future and/or past events are revealing to them.

Demons of Divination are harmless. A person possessed by one of these demons will not be of a physical threat to others by reason of carrying the demon. Demons of Divination operate via persons in different ways. For example: a woman with a Demon of Divination may see future and past occurrences via dreams, and a man with such a demon may see into the future or the unknown by touching.

To invoke and get a Demon of Divination inside of you—so you can foretell—you will have to write the invoking words using Roman numerals. As you may already know, a number can be used to represent a letter. So for example, the word 'spirit' can be written in Roman numerals as Vll Vll lV Vll lV Vlll. How does this work? Take a close look at the following workout:

S...Vll
P...Vll
I...lV
R...Vll
I....lV
T...Vlll

In English, the word 'spirit' would be 7 7 4 7 4 8 and would be explained as follows:

S...7
P...7
I...4
R...7
I...4
T...8

You may not want to attempt this invoking method, because the complete procedure is not laid out herein.

Demons of Destruction

These are the sort of demons which are pernicious in nature. They are extremely potent and carelessly destructive in all their ways. When you invoke a Demon of Destruction, do not let it possesses (enter) you. When a Demon of Destruction possesses a person, it usually causes the person to be dangerous to others and him or herself. When you invoke a Demon of Destruction, you should only make a request on it to act.   You should not ask it to enter you, because it could make you mad. Demons of Destruction can be invoked the same way as Blood Demon, exempting the use of blood.

Dealing with Potions

There are many different potions with different ways of making a lot of them. Notwithstanding the different potions and methods, you should obtain knowledge on many different potions and how they are made in order to deal with situations that require the use of potions. Learning to use potions is like a medical doctor learning to handle medicines. Not all witches learn how to make potions, but it would be a good idea if you do.

When you are learning how to make potions, you should learn:

1. Purpose or purposes of the potion

2. How it should be used

3. Its effect or effects

4. And, if applicable, the antidote against it.

There are different kinds of potions. The different categories include healing potions, spirit repelling potions, love potions, death potions, and good luck potions.

Healing Potion

Healing potions mostly involve the use of herbs. There are two types of healing potions. One type is called 'herbal medicines'. By learning how different plants are used to prevent and cure different illnesses, a witch will be able to make healing potions from such plants.

Healing potions are used, the second way, with spirits. This time they can be called 'spirit potions' and might also involve the use of herbs. By using the effects of spirits with the effects of herbs, you will be able to heal your clients both spiritually and physically. For example, say a woman with a curse is brought before you. The syndromes of the curse on her are madness, foaming from the mouth, and weakness of body. You will handle her madness by instructing one or more of your spirits (ghost or demon) to remove the spirit from the young woman that is making her mad. After that, you will handle her foaming and weakness of body by giving her an herbal medicine to drink. The young woman would be healed both mentally (because you removed the possessing spirit from her) and physically (when you gave her the herbal medicine).

Spirit repelling potions

A spirit repelling potion is a potion that causes a spirit to go away. Depending on the spirit you are dealing with (ghost or demon) you   will use such a potion in an exorcism, a séance, or completely on its own. You can drive away a ghost using only a potion. But to drive away a demon, the potion will have to be used in a ritual of an exorcism or séance.

If a ghost is haunting a place by making on and off appearances or creating weird sounds, you should make a potion that appeases the ghost so that it will go away. A simple potion to use is as follows:

Ingredients

Chicken blood
Crushed garlic pegs

Method

Squeeze the chicken blood into the bottle. You, or the person you give the potion to, must sprinkle the blood in the place the ghost is haunting.

Another way of doing it is to bring the live chicken to the place; kill it and then sprinkle the blood around the place.

Note: If the ghost is acting on its own, it will go away. But if the ghost is acting under the command of another witch, the potion you make will most likely not work. This is because the ghost is under a command. In this case, you have to use another method. If you are already working with a spirit, you should invoke the spirit and instruct it to 'restrain' or drive out the haunting spirit. What do I mean by 'restrain'? You have the option of instructing your spirit to restrain the haunting ghost so that you can use it for your own purposes or lack it away through an incantation.

Protection Potions

As a witch, you can make potions to protect individuals whose lives are in danger. You can make protection potions from anything—such as crushed pieces of dried roots, grave dirt, or a crushed piece of mirror. To make a protection potion, you need two things:

(1) A spirit and

(2) A potion.

It does not matter what you make the potion from. It could merely be dirt tied up in a tiny bag. What makes the tiny bag of dirt a 'protection potion' is a spirit. By connecting a spirit to the potion, you hence have a 'protection potion' that you can give to an individual. By carrying the potion, the individual carries the spirit.

So how a protection potion really works?

Let's say a young man comes to you because his life is in danger—others want to kill him. You can provide him with a protection potion that you can make as follows:

Step 1: Crush a small piece of dried tree root to powder and put it into a tiny bag. This is now the potion.

<u>Step 2:</u> Invoke a spirit and instruct it to guide the carrier of the potion.   Instruct the spirit on how it should notify the carrier (in this case, the young man) of imminent danger at any particular time. The spirit may notify the young man of coming danger by, for example, creating a sense of heat. By carrying the potion, the young man carries the spirit with him wherever he goes.

Instead of using a potion, you can use a ring or necklace. You will simply invoke a spirit and instruct it to guide the carrier of the ring or necklace.

You may not be able to provide this kind of service for free. When you give someone a protection ring, protection necklace, or protection potion-- you are actually sending away one of the spirits you have. It is really the act of 'renting a spirit.' So this should come with a cost. The amount you charge should be reoccurring—like every two years. A protection ring, for example, can cost up to US$3000.

Imprecations

An imprecation is a spoken curse. This however does not mean that an imprecation has to be improvised. An imprecation can first be written to ensure it is succinct. But for an imprecation to be effectual (whether first written or to be improvised) it has to be spoken.

So how is an imprecation constructed?

An imprecation must consist of two parts:

(a) An appeal to a spirit and

(b) Instruction for it to do something.

In simple words, for an imprecation to work, there must be a ghost or demon to carry out what has been spoken. A person with no useful knowledge of ghosts and demons can use an imprecation—if it was already written with the appropriate magical words.

On the next page is an example of an imprecation first written before it is spoken. The imprecation appeals demons to haunt a named person.

Curse of misery

(This imprecation is to cause misery on someone. The name 'John Brown' is used as an example).

Spirit of darkness and of day.
Spirit, humbly hear my plea.
Happiness of John Brown please force away.
Ruin his night, ruin his day.
Bring misery on him wherever he stays.

Instructing Spirits

There are many methods which are used to make requests on and give instructions to spirits. Some witches have developed their own methods to communicate with spirits they use. But most methods used today were carried through generations.

To instruct and make requests on spirits, you must first be cognizant of the kind of spirits you are dealing with. Using a ghost to do something is different from using a demon. A ghost is invoked and instructed. A demon, on the other hand, has to be invoked and a request sedulously made on it—which it might not adhere to.

Here are some instructions used when instructing spirits:

Face to face instruction.

 This is when you are facing a demon, and vice versa, while giving it an instruction—which can be during an invocation or exorcism of a place/person.

Non-vocal instruction

This is any instruction a witch gives to a spirit by doing, rather than saying, things.   Because the witch already has a spirit under his command, the witch will do something he wants to happen to an individual and the ghost will replicate it on the targeted individual.

For example, a witch may gather a needle, a doll, and a photograph of an individual. If he sticks one foot of the doll with the needle, the spirit will affect the foot of the individual in the photograph. If he sticks the belly of the doll, the spirit will affect the belly of the individual in the photograph. Without voicing instruction to the spirit, the witch instructs it to harm or kill the individual in the photograph.

The End

Author's note: Remember, reading this book alone is not enough. You must do the things it says. Where this book gives you an option, make the choice better for you. Remember to post your review on Amazon after reading this book. Let other readers know what you think.

About The Author

Nigel D. Salmon is an author, songwriter, entrepreneur and the founder of Life Support Jamaica. He loves to read and meet new people who share his interests. He lives in St Elizabeth, Jamaica. Website: www.NigeldSalmon.com